VIRGINIA

in words and pictures

BY DENNIS B. FRADIN

ILLUSTRATIONS BY ROBERT ULM

 CHILDRENS PRESS, CHICAGO

Picture Acknowledgments:
VIRGINIA STATE TRAVEL SERVICE-pages 2, 10, 17, 18, 20, 21, 24, 32, 33 (right), 36, 38, 40 (top left)
PENINSULA CHAMBER OF COMMERCE-pages 5 (left), 24 (right), 28 , and front cover
UNITED AIRLINES-pages 5 (right), 16, 17 (right), 19, 30, 31, 32 (left), 40 (bottom and right top)
VIRGINIA STATE LIBRARY-pages 6, 23
VIRGINIA MUSEUM-page 11
DEPARTMENT OF THE NAVY-page 27

Blue Ridge Mountains

1 2 3 4 5 6 7 8 9 10 11 12 R 78 77 76

Library of Congress Cataloging in Publication Data

Fradin, Dennis.
 Virginia, in words and pictures.

 SUMMARY: A simple history of Virginia with
illustrations and a description of its famous
historical sights and cities as they are today.
 1. Virginia—History—Juvenile literature.
|1. Virginia—History| I. Ulm, Robert. II. Title
F226.3.F68   975.5   76-7387
ISBN 0-516-03945-8

"Those mountains *are* blue!"

Like many people you may be surprised when you see the Blue Ridge Mountains in Virginia. This is a beautiful state. It is exciting to think that so much of America's history happened here.

Millions of years ago, there was no state of Virginia.
There was only the land. And for millions of years
the land was under water. The water finally left. Later
mountains rose out of the Earth. No people were
here yet. But there were plenty of dinosaurs. You can
still see dinosaur footprints in Virginia.

The Indians were the first to live here. But it was
the English (ING • lish) explorers who named the land
Virginia.

In 1607 King James of England (ING • land) sent 105 people to live here. They crossed the ocean in three little ships. The people had come to stay. They were called settlers. These settlers built a fort. They named it Jamestown—after King James. Jamestown was the first English settlement in America.

Jamestown Monument

Last remaining original buildings in Jamestown

Captain John Smith

The Indians thought the settlers were outsiders. Often the settlers and the Indians fought each other. The leader of the Jamestown settlers was Captain John Smith. Once, the Indians nearly killed him. Stories say he was saved by an Indian princess, Pocahontas. (po • kah • HAN • tis)

The settlers had other troubles. They didn't know how to farm the land. In 1610 most of them starved to death.

"We must go back to England!" some said.

But the people of Jamestown stayed. In 1612 a man named John Rolfe (RAWLF) showed them how to grow tobacco. The settlers sold the tobacco to England. Now they could buy the things they needed to live.

John Rolfe married Pocahontas, the daughter of the mighty Chief Powhatan (pow • ah • TAN). For a while, the Indians and the settlers got along.

More and more settlers came to Virginia. Some built big houses and became rich growing tobacco. In 1619 the first slaves were brought to work on these tobacco plantations.

Then Chief Powhatan died. The settlers and the Indians began fighting again.

Still more settlers came to Virginia. They came
from many countries. Most were English, but many
came from France (FRANSS). These settlers moved
west and built new towns. The Indians fought, but
they were pushed from their land.

"This is our land!" said the French.

"We rule here!" said the English.

England, France, and the Indians fought over the
land. England won the war. Now England ruled
everyone in Virginia.

Soon after this war many settlers became angry at England. They didn't like the taxes that King George made them pay. These people thought of themselves as Americans. They didn't want to be ruled by England any longer.

The people of America fought against England. This fight was called the Revolutionary War (rev • oh • LOO • shun • airy wore). And many Virginians were leaders. Patrick Henry said, "Give me liberty or give me death." Thomas Jefferson wrote the Declaration of Independence. George Washington became the head of the American army.

Using authentic wooden fifes and rope-tied drums, this unit performs music from the Revolutionary period.

Washington Addressing the Constitutional Convention (By Junius Brutus Stearns)

It wasn't much of an army. The soldiers didn't have enough guns or clothes. One winter they almost starved. But George Washington said they must fight to make a new, free country.

Washington and the American army won the war. On October 18, 1781 England's army gave up at Yorktown, Virginia.

A new country had been born. It was called the United States of America. Virginia became the 10th state in 1788.

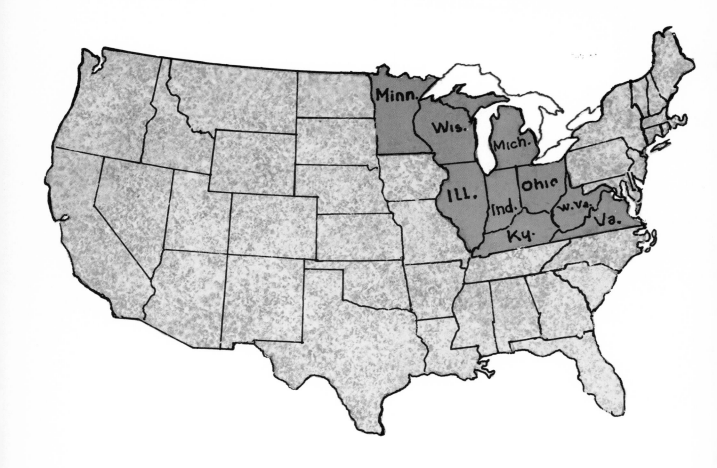

Once Virginia was much bigger than it is now. It was
so big that eight other states were made from it.
Illinois, Indiana, Kentucky, Michigan, Minnesota,
Ohio, West Virginia, and Wisconsin were all once part
of Virginia. That is why Virginia is called the
"Mother of States."

In 1789 George Washington became the first President of the United States. He was the first of eight Virginians who became president. The others were Presidents Jefferson, Madison, Monroe, Harrison, Tyler, Taylor, and Wilson. That is why Virginia is also called the "Mother of Presidents."

During the Civil War the Northern states fought the Southern states. It was a sad time in Virginia. Many Virginians wanted the state to leave the United States. These people didn't want to give up slavery. They wanted their state to be able to do what it wanted.

Other Virginians didn't want to leave the United
States. They didn't like slavery. These Virginians
broke away. They made a new state—West Virginia.

On April 17, 1861 Virginia did leave the United
States. Richmond (RICH • mund), Virginia became the
capital city of the South. Robert E. Lee, a Virginian,
led the southern army.

Hundreds of bloody battles were fought in Virginia.
Fredericksburg, (FRED • ricks • berg) and Spotsylvania

(spot • sill • VAIN • eea) Courthouse, Richmond, and
Manassas (ma • NASS • ez) were places where
thousands of Americans killed each other.

Finally, the South lost. General Lee gave up to the
leader of the northern army, Ulysses (you • LISS • eez) S.
Grant, at Appomattox (ap • ah • MAT • ox), Virginia on
April 9, 1865.

The Civil War, like the Revolutionary War, had
ended in Virginia. Virginia was once again part of the
United States of America.

Jamestown-17th century ships (*Susan Constant*, *Godspeed* and *Discovery*)

The past comes alive when you visit Virginia. You can see the homes of the famous people. You can see the places where so much blood was spilled.

Jamestown is now a National Historical Park. Climb aboard one of these ships on the James River. "They seem so small!" you say. But the first settlers crossed the Atlantic Ocean in ships like these.

Nearby Fort James has been rebuilt. It looks just like it did in 1607. The church where John Rolfe married Pocahontas is still standing.

Take the beautiful Colonial Parkway to Williamsburg. Williamsburg has been rebuilt, too. It looks just like it did two hundred years ago. You feel like you've traveled back in time.

Jamestown fort (restored)

Capitol building-Williamsburg

Street scene in Colonial Williamsburg

Take a buggy ride through the old streets. The
wigmakers and blacksmiths are still at work. The
jail still stands where Blackbeard the pirate was held.
Those cannons were really fired in the
Revolutionary War.

Near Williamsburg there is a huge plantation called
Carter's Grove. This is the way the richest Virginians
lived. Young George Washington and Thomas
Jefferson were often guests here. They ate and danced
in these rooms.

Mount Vernon

One of the most beautiful places in Virginia is
Mount Vernon (VER • nun). This was George
Washington's home. As a young man, Washington
wanted to learn everything about crops and
planting. When the war came, he had to leave Mount
Vernon. He became a great general and the first
President of the United States. But after eight years
as president, Washington was happy to return home.

Mount Vernon-interior

The inside of the house looks as it did when George Washington lived here . . . more than 200 years ago. When you go to Mount Vernon you can see the tomb where "the father of our country" is buried.

Monticello (mon • tih • SELL • oh) is near the center of Virginia. This was the home of Thomas Jefferson. Jefferson wrote the Declaration of Independence. He was our third president. But he did many other things, too.

Monticello

Jefferson was an inventor. He built beds that came out of the wall. He made a seven-day clock for his home.

He also planned the University of Virginia in nearby Charlottesville (SHAR • lots • vill). Thomas Jefferson was almost 80 years old when the university was built. So he stayed at home and looked through his telescope to make sure it was being built right.

Once people thought that tomatoes were poison. Thomas Jefferson proved they weren't by eating one. Think of that the next time you eat a tomato.

Capitol building in Richmond

Virginia is dotted with Civil War battlefields. Visit Appomattox National Park, where the Civil War finally ended. It was near the Courthouse that the Southern soldiers put down their arms.

Visit McLean House, where General Lee met General Grant. So much blood had been spilled. Here at Appomattox, the Civil War finally ended.

Richmond is the capital city of Virginia. The capitol building was planned by Thomas Jefferson.

Turkey farm in Rockingham

NASA research center

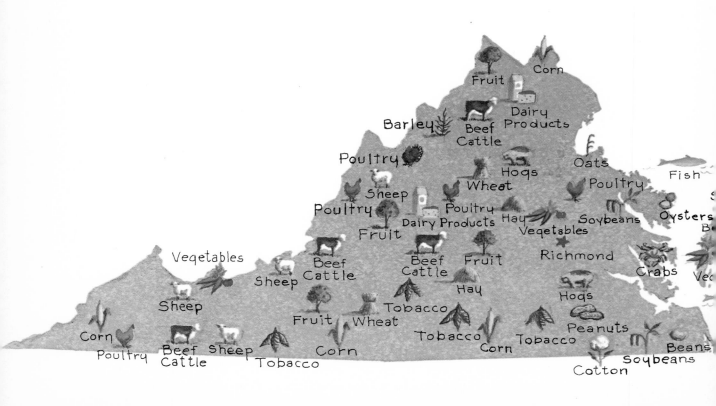

In Richmond there is a museum called the White House of the Confederacy (kahn • FED • er • ah • see). Here you can see Civil War maps, papers, and guns. This building was once the home of Jefferson Davis. He was the President of the Southern, or Confederate, states during the Civil War.

Richmond is a busy city. It has factories that turn out tobacco and medicine.

Today, Virginia is a modern state. Much manufacturing is done in her cities. Chemicals, tobacco, and furniture are some of the leading products.

There's a good chance that the cloth for your clothes came from factories in Virginia.

Norfolk (NOR • fawk) is Virginia's biggest city. The Norfolk Naval Base is the largest in the United States. Navy ships sail into the waters of Chesapeake (CHESS • ah • peek) Bay, then out into the Atlantic Ocean.

Chemicals and machinery are made in Norfolk. Then they go by ship to other cities.

Norfolk is a nice city to visit in the spring. Then the Gardens-by-the-Sea are in bloom.

Nearby Virginia Beach is a place for fun. Here people like to fish and swim.

SH-3 Sea King

Helicopter pilot

U.S.S. Forrestal (CU-59)

Flight deck

P-3 Orion

RA-5C Vigilante landing

Shipbuilding in Newport News

The Mariner's Museum in Newport News

An unusual bridge links Norfolk with a part of Virginia called the Eastern Shore. This bridge is about 23 miles long. Part of it goes under the waters of Chesapeake Bay. Then it is more like a tunnel than a bridge.

In Newport News (NU • port NOOZ) ships are built. The Enterprise (ENTER • prize) was built here. It is a huge aircraft carrier.

The Mariner's Museum is in Newport News. There are thousands of ships here. But these ships aren't real. They are just models.

Arlington Cemetery

Arlington Cemetery-Tomb of the Unknown Soldier

Arlington (ARE • ling • tun), Virginia is very close to
Washington D.C. The Pentagon (PENT • ah • gahn) is in
Arlington. This government building is the largest
office building in the world. More than 27,000 people
work here.

Dulles
International
Airport-
Terminal
exterior

Dulles
International
Airport-
Terminal
interior

Dulles (DUL • iss) International Airport is not very
far from Arlington. This airport is very modern. You
feel you've taken a time machine into the future.

The Transportation Museum in Roanoke

The city of Roanoke (ROE • ah • noke) is in
southwestern Virginia. Clothes and furniture are
made here. Coal is mined in the area. Trains go in and
out of Roanoke. They connect the city to the rest of
Virginia.

Roanoke is sometimes called "the Star City." High
up on Mill Mountain is a big neon star. At night the
star shines over the city. The Mother Goose Zoo is
also on Mill Mountain. This zoo is just for children.

Booker T. Washington National Monument (a cabin) is near Roanoke. Booker T. Washington was born a slave. Later he became a great teacher. He started a college for Blacks. This was when Black people could not go to other colleges.

In many parts of Virginia you won't see cities. The land looks the way it has for ages.

d Grist mill in countryside

Adam Thoroughgood House-oldest brick house in America

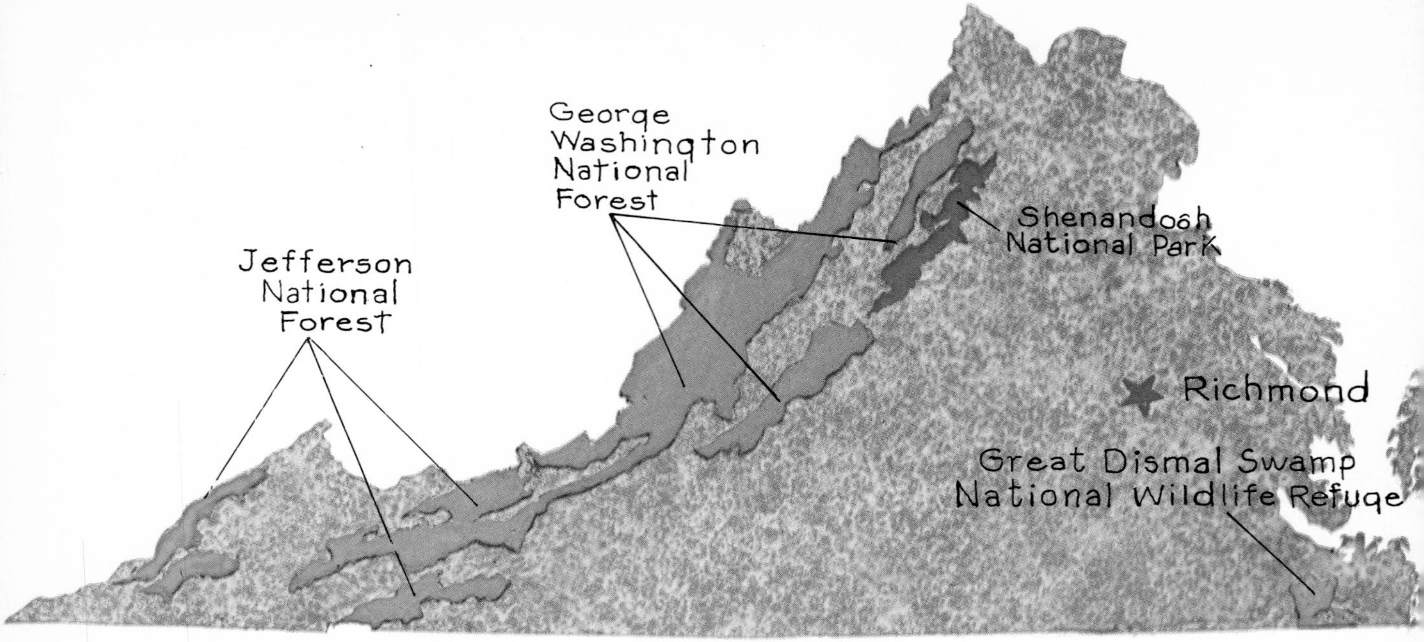

Top map labels:

Jefferson National Forest

George Washington National Forest

Shenandoah National Park

★ Richmond

Great Dismal Swamp National Wildlife Refuge

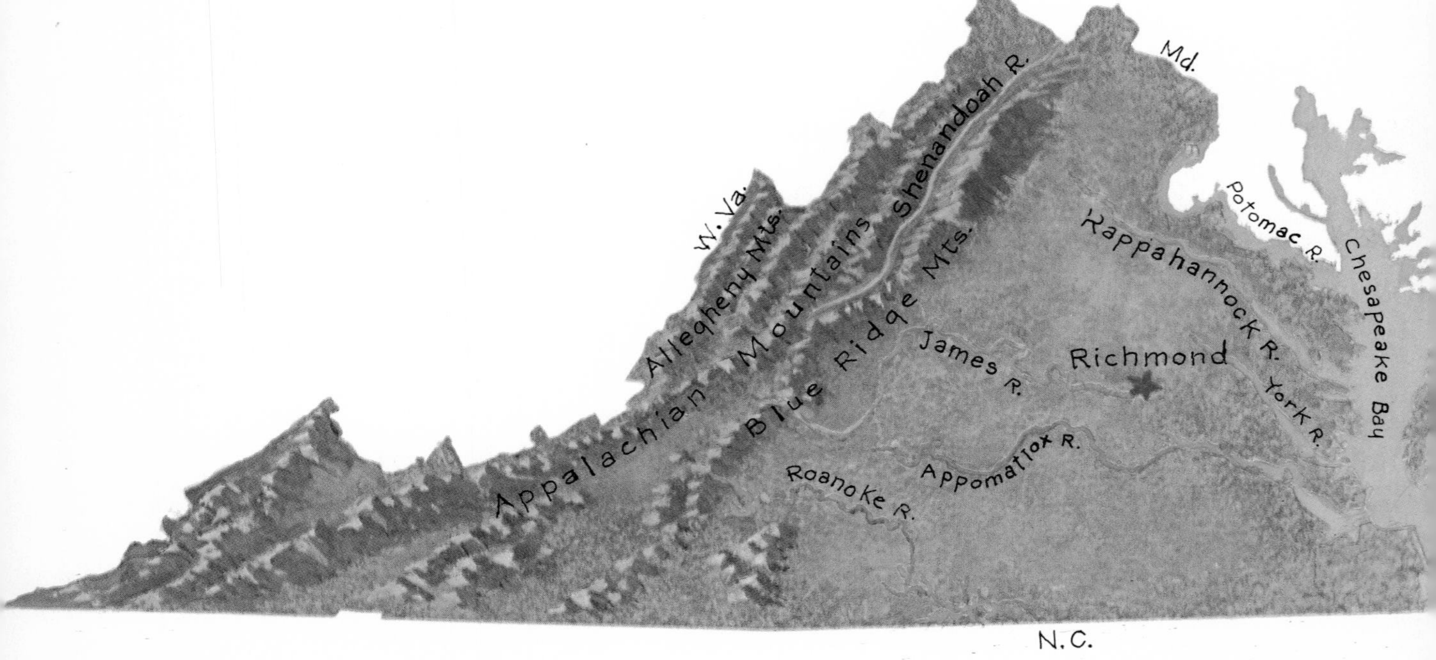

Bottom map labels:

Md.

W. Va.

Allegheny Mts.

Appalachian Mountains

Blue Ridge Mts.

Shenandoah R.

Rappahannock R.

Potomac R.

Chesapeake Bay

York R.

James R.

★ Richmond

Appomattox R.

Roanoke R.

N.C.

There are many mountains in Virginia. The Blue Ridge Mountains and the Allegheny (al • ah • GAY • nee) Mountains are both part of a bigger chain—The Appalachian (apah • LAY • chee • an) Mountains. Mount Rogers is the highest peak in Virginia. It is 5,729 feet high. Virginia has many rivers. The York, James, and Roanoke are just three of Virginia's rivers.

Virginia has six state forests. Pocahontas (po • kah • HAHN • tis) State Forest is southwest of Richmond. This beautiful place is named after the Indian princess, Pocahontas. The forest reminds people of Indian days.

Shenandoah Apple Blossom Festival, Winchester

Dancing at the Shenandoah Apple Blossom Festival

Oyster Festival, Chincoteague

Apple Harvesting, Winchester

17th Street market, Richmond

Many of the foods you eat come from Virginia. Fishermen in Chesapeake Bay catch many kinds of fish. Farmers raise turkeys, chickens, and beef cattle. And people's mouths water when they see Virginia hams.

Apples and peanuts are leading crops. In the spring time, apple trees blossom across the rolling countryside.

Buffalo, wolves, and panthers once roamed Virginia. These animals have been wiped out. But there are still deer and elk in Virginia. Black bears and wildcats are still seen in Dismal Swamp.

Dismal Swamp

Dismal Swamp is southwest of Norfolk. It is a huge
area of wet land. Long ago, escaped prisoners tried
to hide here. But they couldn't live long in the swamp.

Some very famous ponies live in Virginia. These
are the wild ponies of Chincoteague (ching • ka • TEEG)
Island. The ponies are born on a nearby island. But
once a year they are driven across the water to
Chincoteague. On "Pony Penning Day" many of the
ponies are sold.

Virginia has some of the greatest natural wonders in the world.

Most bridges are built by people. Natural Bridge near Lexington (LEK • sing • tun) was not. It was cut out of stone by the creek that runs two hundred feet below. The Indians called it the "Bridge of God." Once, it was owned by Thomas Jefferson.

In the western part of Virginia there are many caves and underground caverns. Indians stopped to rest in these caves as they moved across the land. It is thought that runaway slaves hid in caves as they fled to the North.

The seven Natural Chimneys are thin rock towers. These chimneys are as tall as ten-story buildings.

Mennonite buggy in Shenandoah Valley

Shenandoah Valley

Shenandoah Valley-Fall colors along road

Shenandoah Valley in fall

Natural Tunnel, 900 feet long, was carved through a mountain by wind and water. Now, it is used as a railroad tunnel.

Before you leave Virginia, stop at famous Shenandoah (shen • an • DOE • ah) National Park. The Shenandoah Valley is one of the most beautiful places in the world. The Indians called it the "Daughter of the Stars." Once, George Washington owned land here.

Virginia is . . .

Jamestown, Yorktown, Williamsburg

Mount Vernon, Monticello

Home of 8 Presidents

Mother of States

Virginia is a place of living beauty and living history.

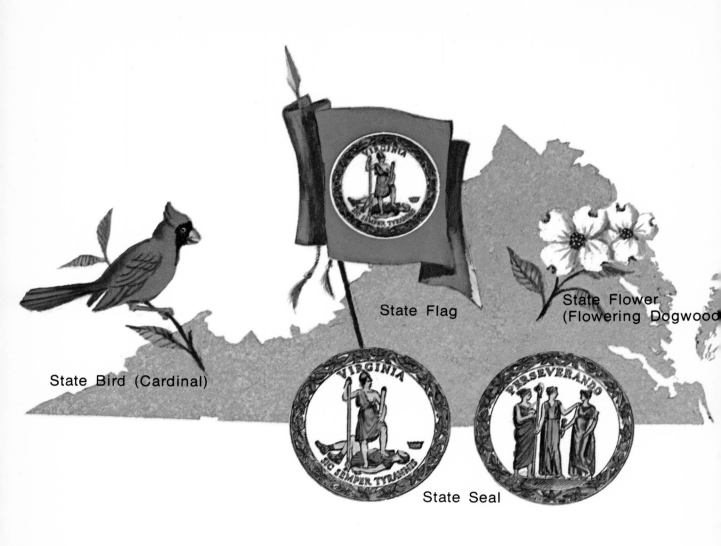

State Flag

State Flower
(Flowering Dogwood)

State Bird (Cardinal)

State Seal

Facts About VIRGINIA

Area—40,817 square miles ranked 36

Highest Point—5,729 (Mount Rogers)

Lowest Point—Sea Level

Temperature Extremes—high: 110° (Balcony Falls); low: minus 29° (Monterey)

Statehood—10th state, June 25, 1788

Counties—95

U.S. Senators—2

U.S. Representatives—10

Capital—Richmond, founded 1737

State Song—"Carry Me Back to Old Virginia" by James A. Bland
State Motto—*Sic Semper Tyrannis* (Thus always (ever) to Tyrants)
Familiar Name—Old Dominion
Nickname—Mother of Presidents
Agricultural Products—tobacco, peanuts, apples, sweet potatoes, soybeans, corn, vegetables, peaches, barley, turkeys, beef cattle, hogs
Population—4,936,000 (U.S. est. 1975)
Population Density—121 persons per square mile

Major Cities—	
Norfolk	307,951
Richmond	249,431
Arlington	174,284
Virginia Beach	172,106
Newport News	138,177
Hampton	120,779
Portsmouth	110,963
Alexandria	110,927

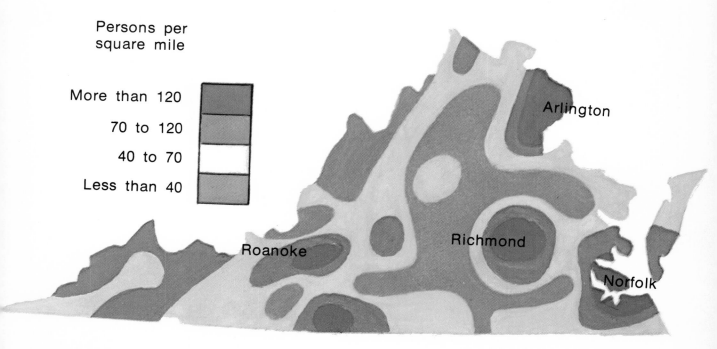

Persons per square mile

More than 120
70 to 120
40 to 70
Less than 40

Manufacturing Industries—chemicals, textiles,
food products, clothing, lumber furniture, paper
products
Minerals—Coal is number one (70%), lime zinc,
stone, cement

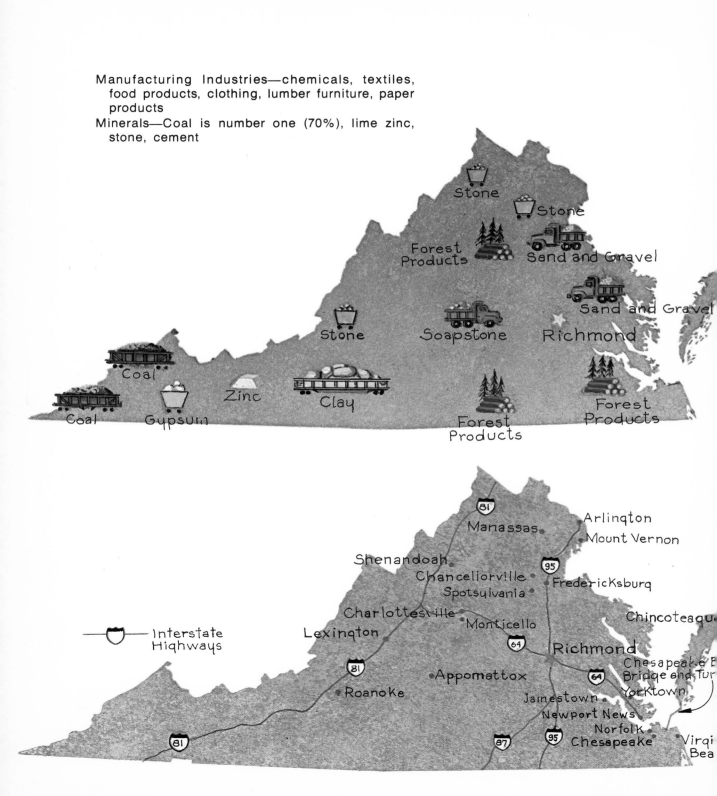

Stone

Stone

Forest
Products

Sand and Gravel

Sand and Gravel

Stone

Soapstone

Richmond

Coal

Zinc

Clay

Coal

Gypsum

Forest
Products

Forest
Products

Interstate
Highways

81

Manassas

Arlington

Mount Vernon

Shenandoah

95

Chancellorville

Fredericksburg

Spotsulvania

Charlottesville

Chincoteagu

Lexington

Monticello

64

Richmond

81

Appomattox

64

Chesapeake B
Bridge and Tur

Roanoke

Jamestown

Yorktown

Newport News

Norfolk

81

87

95

Chesapeake

Virgi
Bea

Virginia History

1497—Cabot explores area for England.

1607—Colony of Jamestown established.

1609—John Smith returns to England.

1610—Jamestown starving.

1612—John Rolfe plants tobacco for sale in England.

1618—Chief Powhatan dies.

1619—Oldest American legislature—House of Burgesses—begins. Dutch traders bring the first Negroes to Jamestown.

1622—Great massacre by Indians.

1624—Virginia becomes a royal colony.

1693—College of William and Mary opens.

1699—Capital moves to Williamsburg.

1716—Governor Spotswood explores the western lands.

1732—George Washington is born.

1736—Patrick Henry is born.

1737—Richmond founded.

1743—Thomas Jefferson is born.

1751—James Madison is born.

1758—James Monroe is born.

1763—French and Indian War ends.

1773—Virginia Committee of Correspondence set up; William Henry Harrison born.

1775—George Washington becomes commander in chief of the Continental Army.

1776—Virginia declares itself free; Thomas Jefferson writes the Declaration of Independence.

1779—Richmond becomes capital.

1781—The British surrender at Yorktown (the last battle of the Revolutionary War).

1788—Statehood.

1790—First canal in country opened from Richmond to Westham.

1792—Original portion of Capitol completed; Kentucky is made out of three of Virginia's western counties.

1799—George Washington and Patrick Henry die.

1801-1825—Three Virginians become president: Thomas Jefferson (1801-1809), James Madison (1809-1817), James Monroe (1817-1825).

1818—University of Virginia chartered.

1826—Thomas Jefferson dies.

1831—James Monroe dies; McCormick invents the reaper.

1836—James Madison dies.

1841—William Henry Harrison becomes President and dies a month later. Vice-President John Tyler becomes President.

1856—Thomas Woodrow Wilson born.

1861—Virginia leaves the Union, Civil War begins.

1863—West Virginia becomes a state.

1865—Lee surrenders; Civil War ends.

1902—New state constitution.

1912—Woodrow Wilson becomes the eighth Virginian to be elected President.

1917—World War I begins.

1924— Woodrow Wilson dies.

1927—State government reorganized.

1935—Shenandoah National Park established.

1941—World War II begins.

1966—State Department of Community Colleges established.

1964—The Chesapeake Bay Bridge-Tunnel opens.

1971—New state constitution.

About the Author:

Dennis Fradin attended Northwestern University on a creative writing scholarship and graduated in 1967. While still at Northwestern, he published his first stories in *Ingenue* magazine and also won a prize in *Seventeen's* short story competition. A prolific writer, Dennis Fradin has been regularly publishing stories in such diverse places as *The Saturday Evening Post, Scholastic, National Humane Review, Midwest,* and *The Teaching Paper.* He has also scripted several educational films. Since 1970 he has taught second grade reading in a Chicago school—a rewarding job, which, the author says, "provides a captive audience on whom I test my children's stories." Married and the father of two children, Dennis Fradin spends his free time with his family or playing a myriad of sports and games with his childhood chums.

About the Artist:

Robert Ulm, a Chicago resident, has been an advertising and editorial artist in both New York and Chicago. Mr. Ulm is a successful painter as well as an illustrator. In his spare time he enjoys fishing and playing tennis.